To all the strong, curious, brilliant girls and young women who are out there making the world a better place, especially Maddison Stemple-Piatt, Hannah Brooks, and Maddi Wise—**H. E. Y. S.**

To my mother, who taught me to be a strong and independent woman—**E. P.**

Published by Charlesbridge
9 Galen Street
Watertown, MA 02472
(617) 926-0329
www.charlesbridge.com

Printed in China
(hc) 10 9 8 7 6 5 4 3 2 1

Library of Congress Cataloging-in-Publication Data
Names: Stemple, Heidi E. Y., author. | Paik, Emily, illustrator.
Title: She sells seashells: Mary Anning, an unlikely paleontologist / Heidi E. Y. Stemple; illustrated by Emily Paik.
Description: Watertown, MA: Charlesbridge, [2024] | Includes bibliographical references. | Audience: Ages 5–9 | Audience: Grades 2–3 | Summary: "In the early 1800s, Mary Anning was a young girl who collected fossils and shells on the seaside cliffs by her home; and even though she was a most unlikely scientist, Mary eventually made significant fossilized discoveries that paved the way for the development of the field of paleontology."—Provided by publisher.
Identifiers: LCCN 2023013236 (print) | LCCN 2023013237 (ebook) | ISBN 9781623543280 (hardcover) | ISBN 9781632899958 (ebook)
Subjects: LCSH: Anning, Mary, 1799–1847—Juvenile literature. | Women paleontologists—England—Biography—Juvenile literature. | Paleontologists—England—Biography—Juvenile literature. | Fossils—Juvenile literature. | Paleontology—Juvenile literature.
Classification: LCC QE707.A56 S74 2024 (print) | LCC QE707.A56 (ebook) | DDC 560.92 [B]—dc23/eng/20231002
LC record available at https://lccn.loc.gov/2023013236
LC ebook record available at https://lccn.loc.gov/2023013237

Illustrations done in digital media
Display type set in Gable Antique Condensed Regular by Jim Spiece and ITC Fenice by Aldo Novarese
Text type set in Crimson Text by Sebastian Kosch and Fjala One by Irina Smirnova
Printed by 1010 Printing International Limited in Huizhou, Guangdong, China
Production supervision by Mira Kennedy
Designed by Jon Simeon

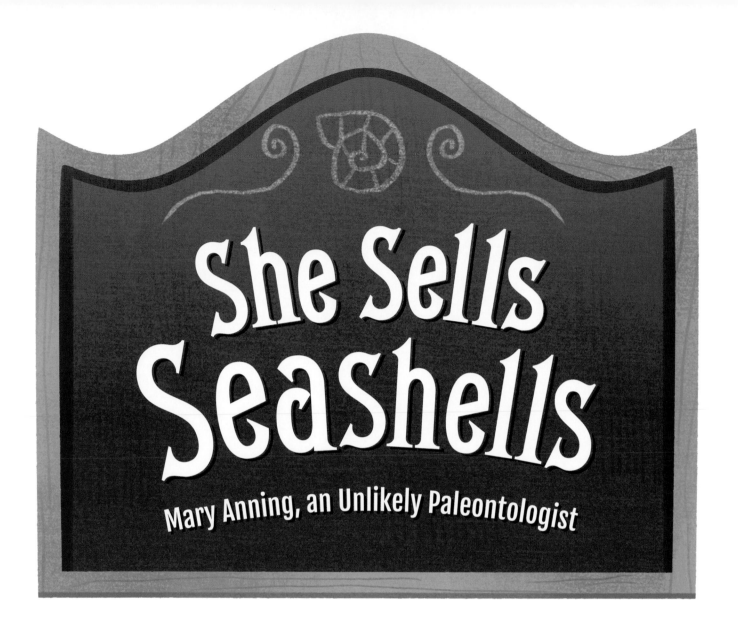

She Sells Seashells

Mary Anning, an Unlikely Paleontologist

Heidi E. Y. Stemple

Illustrated by **Emily Paik**

Charlesbridge

She sells seashells by the seashore.
The shells she sells are seashells, I'm sure.
For if she sells seashells on the seashore,
Then I'm sure she sells seashore shells.

Mary Anning was an unlikely paleontologist. Especially unlikely for England in the early 1800s.

In fact, Mary wasn't a paleontologist at all. She was just a girl—a girl who collected fossilized seashells and other curiosities and sold them in her family's shop.

Mary had good eyes and clever hands.
Mary had strong tools.
And Mary had remarkable patience.

Chip! Scrape! Chip!

Mary and her brother worked side by side along the seaside cliffs near their home. Their father had taught them to spot treasures in the layers of limestone and shale. But it was Mary who toiled for hours, days, and months, teasing fossils—shell, tooth, and bone—out of the rugged terrain. She could feel where the rock was hiding something special. The pick her father made for her before he died fit perfectly in her small hands.

What Mary didn't have was an education.

Mary had neither the time nor money for school. Selling the fossils she collected helped put food on her family's table. One fossil at a time. One meal at a time.

Though she was curious to learn about her discoveries, she was just a girl.

Back then, girls could collect pretty or peculiar things, but rarely did they get to study them. And girls from poor families certainly didn't become *scientists*.

Meanwhile, the rich boys of England *were* becoming scientists. They were in fancy schools, getting fancy educations. They earned titles and degrees and worked in respected colleges and important museums.

But Mary didn't worry much about those rich boys.

She was too busy climbing crumbling cliffs and dodging falling rocks in search of new fossils. She wouldn't stop for the day until the incoming tide threatened to pull her out to sea.

Chip! Scrape! Chip!

It was Mary's brother who found a skull in the cliffside. He worked a little, but gave up. Mary took over. First she unearthed vertebrae. Next ribs. Then flippers, and finally a long tail.

Word got out about the extraordinary fossil in Mary's family's shop.

What creature had she uncovered? When a rich man purchased the fossil, Mary used the money to pay her family's rent and buy food. Though she would have liked to learn about those bones, she went right back to doing what was best for her family—finding more fossils.

Grand and educated men set out to identify Mary's creature. They proposed that it was both fish and lizard—a sea dragon of sorts. They preached that it must be from an exotic, faraway land. They debated endlessly about what it meant for their understanding of the world.

The men eventually named this discovery *Ichthyosaur*, and proudly claimed their new knowledge in articles, books, and sermons. The *Ichthyosaur* made it clear that the history of life on Earth was far more expansive than these men had once thought.

No one asked what Mary thought.

But Mary didn't worry much about those educated men.

She was too busy beginning to educate herself.
She read—over and over again—the few books
and scientific journals she could find.

Mary copied the illustrations to learn the technique of cataloging bones and reporting discoveries. She taught herself anatomy by dissecting squid and cuttlefish on her kitchen table.

Little by little, lesson by lesson, an uneducated girl from a poor family was becoming a scientist.

More rich folks—collectors, geologists, and scientists—purchased Mary's fossils and brought them to museums and universities to be studied and displayed. The men who studied them were lauded as scientific heroes.

But Mary didn't worry much about those rich folk.

She was too busy continuing to learn, work, and, provide
for her family. As Mary grew into a young woman, she soon
made another exciting discovery.

One bone led to another. And another. And another. This was no *Ichthyosaur*! It had a long neck—a very long neck—a tiny head, and paddles. Mary worked for months to release this odd fossil from the rocky seaside cliff.

What creature had Mary uncovered *this time*?

The educated men convened a meeting about this revelation. It was fantastic! But had Mary truly found a new species? Or was she accidently mixing the bones of two or more creatures? Was she trying to fool them for money or fame?

The men debated a long time—a very long time—and finally concluded that Mary's bones were from one very real, very new species. They named it *Plesiosaur*.

Of course, no one asked Mary to join the discussion.

Still, Mary didn't worry much about those debating men.

She kept learning on her own. She kept working by the seashore, searching and digging. Next she discovered . . . a diamond-shaped tail. Claws and a beak. And wings— wings! Mary had found one of the first pterosaurs.

Mary's *Ichthyosaur*, *Plesiosaur*, and now *Pterosaur* suddenly inspired new theories about life on Earth long ago. The men congratulated themselves on their study of these fossils and prehistoric life. They were forming a brand-new science—*paleontology*. Did they think to include Mary? No. Of course not.

But, two hundred years later . . .

Mary Anning is recognized as the first paleontologist. The world knows all about the girl who collected fossilized shells and other curiosities to sell in her family's shop.

Chip! Scrape! Chip!

One fossil at a time.

One discovery at a time.

Mary changed the scientific world forever. An unlikely paleontologist forged a path for every girl. For *everyone* curious enough to keep digging.

She Sells

Mary Anning was born on May 21, 1799. Her father was a carpenter who found fossils in his spare time. Back then, he didn't know they were prehistoric relics. Mary's family sold these "curiosities" to people visiting the seashore. At the time people thought that the sea—and the curiosities— could cure sickness.

Despite providing invaluable fossils to scientists in the budding fields of geology and paleontology, Mary and her family lived in poverty most of their lives. Some of her fossil finds brought in money that sustained the family for long periods of time; other times were quite lean.

Mary died in 1847. After her death, she was honored in a speech by the president of the Geological Society of London—a community where men congregated to discuss and advance lofty scientific subjects. Mary hadn't been allowed to join. In fact, the organization didn't admit any women until seventy-two years later, in 1919.

The tongue twister "She Sells Seashells" is adapted from many like it, which dated back before Mary was even born ("Sally Sells," "He sells"). But it was first written down in a song by Terry Sullivan in 1908. From this song, the tongue twister became colloquial—something practically every English-speaking child repeated. It is widely believed, but unproved, of course, that when this tongue twister was changed to "She Sells," the "she" referred to a legendary girl in England who collected fossilized shells and other curiosities. Yes, Mary Anning herself.

Seashells

Mary found and sold fossilized "seashells," including many ammonites—one of which she sold for enough money to feed her family for a whole week. But her more important discoveries were the fossils of the larger prehistoric creatures, beginning with the *Ichthyosaur*. At first she thought these discoveries were more important only because they were worth more money. But because Mary was a smart, curious girl, she began educating herself. In addition to reading and dissecting, Mary asked questions of the people who came to buy her fossils. She eventually learned why fossils were important. Her discoveries painted a picture of the past, and forced scientists to consider new ideas about extinction and evolution.

ICHTHYOSAUR: Ranging from about two feet to more than eighty feet long—with paddle-like fins to propel through water, large eyes to see in dark depths, and sharp teeth for eating sea creatures—this long-jawed aquatic reptile ruled the oceans for about one hundred million years. It became extinct nearly twenty-five million years before the dinosaurs did.

PLESIOSAUR: This giant carnivorous, aquatic reptile is most recognizable by its long neck. At the end of up to seventy-six vertebrae (humans have thirty-three), the plesiosaur's arrow-shaped head was small in comparison to its large body. Propelled by four large paddle-like fins, this creature flew through the water, only to return to the surface between dives to breathe.

PTEROSAUR/PTERODACTYL: These winged lizards had hollow bones like modern birds, and most of the more than two hundred types (including Pterodactyl) could fly. Their wings were made of a membrane (containing muscle, blood vessels, and fibrous cords) attached between the shoulder and ankle, more like bats than birds. Their wingspans ranged from about ten inches to forty feet. Depending on their size, they ate a variety of diets, including meat, fish, and insects.

Mary also found and sold:

AMMONITES: This prehistoric carnivorous marine mollusk was related to octopus, squid, and cuttlefish. An ammonite moved by propelling jets of water through its tube-like body. It lived inside a coiled shell that the mollusk was constantly growing. Though ammonites varied in size, some could grow as large as three feet. They became extinct sixty-five million years ago and are one of the most common fossils found.

BELEMNITES: This prehistoric creature had a squid-like body and a hard, bullet-shaped internal skeleton. It's this strong skeleton called a rostrum that fossil hunters generally find. Because it is a common fossil, the belemnite is very important to scientists. It has helped determine factors such as climate and the direction of the currents of the ocean more than two hundred million years ago.

COPROLITES: Believe it or not, these fossilized feces (that's a fancy word for poop) gave Mary (and a host of scientists) great information about what prehistoric creatures ate. In order to get to that information, Mary had to first turn the rock back into poop by soaking it in a specialized solution. Yes, it's as gross (and stinky) as it sounds.

By the Seashore

The cliffs of the Jurassic seashore, where Mary lived, were underwater when prehistoric creatures populated the Earth two hundred million years ago. As time shifted the landscape and sea levels, much of what was below the sea became uncovered land above. The layers of limestone and shale that make up these cliffs were filled with fossilized remains. With each storm, new fossils were exposed. Mary was skilled in fossil hunting, but she was also lucky to have grown up in an area where there was an abundance of treasure to be discovered.

Today Lyme Regis, in the county of Dorset, is part of a World Heritage Site called the Jurassic Coast. The cliffs still hold treasures to be discovered. People still travel there to hunt for fossils on their own, or often with the help of a hired guide.

The Men

Many smart men were digging and collecting fossils at the same time as Mary. But they were also in museums, laboratories, and lecture halls where Mary wasn't invited. The men were able to take what Mary found; study, hypothesize, and write about her discoveries; and then present them to the world. Back then, Mary wasn't allowed to participate in the meetings of the Geological Society, let alone be a member. No woman was.

These weren't bad men. Many of them considered Mary a colleague and, privately, gave her credit. But she was almost never given public credit—especially for her early finds when she was just a young girl. That credit went to the men.

Perhaps the most important man in Mary's life was the one who, when he realized Mary and her family were struggling, sold his entire collection of fossils and gave every bit of the money to her. Many of the fossils he sold were ones he had originally purchased from Mary. In the pages of history books, you can find the name of this man and the others. But this is Mary's book, so in these pages the men have been left nameless—like Mary had been for much of her career.

Another Mary

Meanwhile, about one hundred fifty miles to the east, right around the same time Mary Anning was unearthing the *Plesiosaur*, another Mary—Mary Ann Mantell—was digging around, too. She found a huge fossilized reptilian tooth, which led to the discovery of the first *Iguanodon*. Was this Mary given credit? Of course not. Her husband got the credit. But that, as they say, is another story entirely. . . .